Greater Than a Tourist Book Series Reviews from Readers

I think the series is wonderful and beneficial for tourists to get information before visiting the city.

-Seckin Zumbul, Izmir Turkey

I am a world traveler who has read many trip guides but this one really made a difference for me. I would call it a heartfelt creation of a local guide expert instead of just a guide.

-Susy, Isla Holbox, Mexico

New to the area like me, this is a must have!

-Joe, Bloomington, USA

This is a good series that gets down to it when looking for things to do at your destination without having to read a novel for just a few ideas.

-Rachel, Monterey, USA

Good information to have to plan my trip to this destination.

-Pennie Farrell, Mexico

Aptly titled, you won't just be a tourist after reading this book. You'll be greater than a tourist!

-Alan Warner, Grand Rapids, USA

Thank you for a fantastic book.

-Don, Philadelphia, USA

Laura Andrews

Great ideas for a port day.
-Mary Martin USA

Even though I only have three days to spend in San Miguel in an upcoming visit, I will use the author's suggestions to guide some of my time there. An easy read - with chapters named to guide me in directions I want to go.
-Robert Catapano, USA

Great insights from a local perspective! Useful information and a very good value!
-Sarah, USA

This series provides an in-depth experience through the eyes of a local. Reading these series will help you to travel the city in with confidence and it'll make your journey a unique one.
-Andrew Teoh, Ipoh, Malaysia

Tourists can get an amazing "insider scoop" about a lot of places from all over the world. While reading, you can feel how much love the writer put in it.
-Vanja Živković, Sremski Karlovci, Serbia

>TOURIST

GREATER THAN A TOURIST – STOCKHOLM SWEDEN

50 Travel Tips from a Local

Laura Andrews

Laura Andrews

Greater Than a Tourist- Stockholm Sweden Copyright © 2018 by CZYK Publishing LLC. All Rights Reserved.

All rights reserved. No part of this book may be reproduced in any form or by any electronic or mechanical means including information storage and retrieval systems, without permission in writing from the author. The only exception is by a reviewer, who may quote short excerpts in a review.

Cover designed by: Ivana Stamenković
Cover image: https://pixabay.com/en/stockholm-sweden-city-urban-1824368/

Greater Than a Tourist
Visit our website at www.GreaterThanaTourist.com

Lock Haven, PA
All rights reserved.

ISBN: 9781980788102

>TOURIST
50 TRAVEL TIPS FROM A LOCAL

Laura Andrews

BOOK DESCRIPTION

Are you excited about planning your next trip?
Do you want to try something new?
Would you like some guidance from a local?

If you answered yes to any of these questions, then this Greater Than a Tourist book is for you.

Greater Than A Tourist – Stockholm, Sweden by Laura Andrews offers the inside scoop on Sweden's capital. Most travel books tell you how to travel like a tourist. Although there is nothing wrong with that, as part of the Greater Than a Tourist series, this book will give you travel tips from someone who has lived at your next travel destination.

In these pages, you will discover advice that will help you throughout your stay. This book will not tell you exact addresses or store hours but instead will give you excitement and knowledge from a local that you may not find in other smaller print travel books.

Travel like a local. Slow down, stay in one place, and get to know the people and the culture. By the time you finish this book, you will be eager and prepared to travel to your next destination.

Laura Andrews

>TOURIST

TABLE OF CONTENTS

BOOK DESCRIPTION
TABLE OF CONTENTS
DEDICATION
ABOUT THE AUTHOR
HOW TO USE THIS BOOK
FROM THE PUBLISHER
OUR STORY
WELCOME TO
> TOURIST
INTRODUCTION
1. Learn The Art Of Lagom
2. Get to Grips With Fika
3. Sing Snapsvisor In The Summer Sun
4. Wrap Up Warm For Winter
5. Decide Where To Stay
6. Get Into The City
7. Get Around Like A Local
8. Take In The History, Culture And Glamour Of Norrmalm And Östermalm
9. Find A Restaurant To Suit Your Taste On Rörstrandgatan
10. Enjoy Cocktails In The Courtyard In Stureplan
11. Lounge Around At Lydmar Hotel
12. Dare To Take A Ghost Walk Through The Old Town
13. Enjoy A Cosy Meal At Stockholms Gastabud
14. Climb The Town Hall Tower
15. Relax By The Lake At Norr Mälarstrand

Laura Andrews

16. Hang Out At Hornsbergstrand
17. Enjoy The Summer Outdoors At Solstugan
18. Challenge Your Friends At Boulebar And Ugglan
19. Play It Cool In Södermalm
20. Stroll Through Södermalm
21. Continue The Stroll Through Södermalm
22. Dinner And A Movie At Bio Rio
23. Brunch Or More At Kvarnen
24. Check Out A Photography Exhibition At Fotografiska
25. Eat Vegetarian Food With A View At Hermans
26. Walk In History's Footsteps Down Fjällgatan
27. Watch The Sun Set Over The City At Mossebacketerassen
28. Eat Traditional Swedish Food At Pelikan
29. Party Under The Bridge
30. Climb Skinnarvik Mountain
31. Go Vegan With Lunch At Mahalo
32. Keep An Eye Out For Benny From ABBA At Hotel Rival
34. Escape The City On The Prison Island
35. Walk Around Djurgården
36. Get Familiar With Nordic Culture And Wildlife At Skansen
37. Ride A Rollercoaster To Live Music At Gröna Lund
38. Be Overwhelmed By Cake At Kaknäs Tower
39. See Where Nobel Experimented With Dynamite
40. Go Hiking In Tyresta National Park
41. Experience Life In The Archipelago
42. Take A Boat Trip To Fjäderholmarna
43. See The Fortress At Vaxholm
44. Fika With A History At Vete-Katten And Gunnarsons
45. Spice Things Up With Two Thai Restaurants

>TOURIST

46. Do Saturday Night Like A Swede
47. Buy Souvenirs
48. Learn Something For Free At One Of Many Museums
49. Embrace Your Inner Tourist
50. Learn Swedish

TOP REASONS TO BOOK THIS TRIP
> TOURIST
GREATER THAN A TOURIST
> TOURIST
GREATER THAN A TOURIST
NOTES

>TOURIST

DEDICATION

This book is dedicated to my family in the UK who gave me the support and confidence I needed to move, all alone, to a strange new country, and to my friends in Sweden who have made this place feel like home.

An extra special thanks goes to Rikard (Stockholm-loving local) and Pinh (eternal tourist) for their valuable help with this project.

Laura Andrews

ABOUT THE AUTHOR

Laura Andrews is originally from the UK, but from an early age had an unusual obsession with all things Nordic. She has travelled from Iceland to Finland and everything in between, but knew the second she stepped foot in Sweden that it was home. Laura subsequently moved to Stockholm in 2014. She has been enjoying exploring the city and embracing Swedish culture ever since.

Laura Andrews

HOW TO USE THIS BOOK

The Greater Than a Tourist book series was written by someone who has lived in an area for over three months. The goal of this book is to help travelers either dream or experience different locations by providing opinions from a local. The author has made suggestions based on their own experiences. Please do your own research before traveling to the area in case the suggested places are unavailable.

Laura Andrews

FROM THE PUBLISHER

Traveling can be one of the most important parts of a person's life. The anticipation and memories that you have are some of the best. As a publisher of the Greater Than a Tourist book series, as well as the popular 50 Things to Know book series, we strive to help you learn about new places, spark your imagination, and inspire you. Wherever you are and whatever you do I wish you safe, fun, and inspiring travel.

Lisa Rusczyk Ed. D.
CZYK Publishing

Laura Andrews

OUR STORY

Traveling is a passion of the "Greater than a Tourist" series creator. Lisa studied abroad in college, and for their honeymoon Lisa and her husband toured Europe. During her travels to Malta, an older man tried to give her some advice based on his own experience living on the island since he was a young boy. She was not sure if she should talk to the stranger but was interested in his advice. When traveling to some places she was wary to talk to locals because she was afraid that they weren't being genuine. Through her travels, Lisa learned how much locals had to share with tourists. Lisa created the "Greater Than a Tourist" book series to help connect people with locals. A topic that locals are very passionate about sharing.

Laura Andrews

>TOURIST

WELCOME TO
> TOURIST

Laura Andrews

>TOURIST

INTRODUCTION

*"He is truly wise
who's travelled far
and knows the ways of the world
He who has travelled
can tell what spirit
governs the men he meets"
- from the Hávamál, book of Viking wisdom.*

The first words on the lips of any tourist visiting Sweden are usually ABBA and IKEA. Luckily Stockholm does not disappoint on either of these fronts. ABBA fans can treat themselves to a trip to the ABBA museum, while IKEA fans can hop on the free bus to the largest IKEA store in the world (make sure you go on the weekend after the 25th of the month, when Swedes get paid, to ensure the ultimate Swedish shopping experience). However, ABBA and IKEA aside, Stockholm is one of the most beautiful capital cities in the world, and as Swedes are happy to pay taxes to keep the city clean, it is always a pleasure to wander around and explore.

As is the case for many places with such a northerly location, Stockholm is a city with two identities. In the summer, everyone heads outside to enjoy the sun after a seemingly endless winter. At this time of year, when they're not swimming in the lake or out on a boat, you'll find Stockholmers in any patch of sun they can find, while restaurants put out tables and chairs on every stretch of pavement. Not a moment

Laura Andrews

is to be spent indoors. Winter, on the other hand, brings the opportunity to watch the snow fall from cosy cafes with candles lighting up every window, or to wrap up warm and go ice skating on the frozen lakes.

For English speakers, there is no need to worry about things getting lost in translation when you're ordering your meatballs (köttbullar) and pickled herring (surströmming), as Sweden is ranked third in the world in the English Proficiency Index. Although if you do want to try your hand at Swedish, the Foreign Service Institute ranks it as one of the easiest languages for native English speakers to learn and it should only take around 600 hours before you are generally proficient. Lycka till!

>TOURIST

1. Learn The Art Of Lagom

"Varken för mycket eller för litet, bara lagom"
Neither too much nor too little, just right

Sweden is a liberal, egalitarian country and Swedish society can often be summed up in one word; lagom. Roughly translated as "just enough or in moderation", lagom is evident in Swedish society through the general belief that no one person should stand out too much. As a result, any extreme outbursts can make Swedes uncomfortable and bring subtle, disapproving glares.

Sweden consistently appears at the top of several international rankings on gender equality and in the top 10 on global happiness scales, while also ranking in the top 10 on global competitiveness. Add all of this together with a comprehensive welfare state and you can see why Swedes are so proud of their society and why other Western countries often look to Sweden as an example when making new policies.

However, with all this measured behaviour, Swedes can sometimes seem rude or stand offish. Try not to be offended, it's just that Swedes are not good at openly showing emotions. In fact they really are friendly underneath, so strike up a conversation, you'll find many Swedes are all too happy to practice their already remarkable English skills.

Swedes are also not known for their spontaneity and so have probably already made their restaurant plans for the next week. That means you should too, if you've got your heart set on eating at a specific place.

It's also worth knowing that this futuristic utopia of Sweden, and particularly Stockholm, is virtually a cashless society. It's therefore sensible to make sure you have a means of paying by card, as you may find some places (some bars, shops and public transport) where it is not possible to pay by cash.

2. Get to Grips With Fika

"Ska vi fika?"
Should we have coffee and a cake?

Fika, loosely translated, means to have a coffee break, but of course no coffee break would be complete without cake, and plenty of it. Fika is an integral part of Swedish society and can be practiced several times a day. If, during your trip, you don't try some quintessential Swedish treats, washed down with a mug of coffee, then you can't say that you've truly experienced Swedish culture. The Swedes have a cake for every occasion, so no matter what your taste you can be sure to find something to tickle your fancy.

Shrove Tuesday (Fettisdag), celebrated at the end of February/beginning of March and the preceding and proceeding

>TOURIST

weeks, means an abundance of semlor. These are buns with the top cut off, filled with almond paste and cream and sometimes eaten in a bowl of hot milk.

Cinnamon buns (kanelbullar) are a quintessential part of fika and Swedes have been eating them in their current form since 1920. There is even a cinnamon bun day, celebrated every year on October 4. If you only have time for one fika during your visit, it should include a cinnamon bun. However, if cinnamon isn't to your taste, a cardamom version (kardemummabullar) is very popular and extremely delicious.

Lucia celebrations, on December 13, represent light and warmth in the middle of a long, dark winter and also mean it's time for saffron buns (lussekatter or lussebullar). You can swap the coffee on this occasion for glögg, which is similar to mulled wine, but a little sweeter.

If you don't have a sweet tooth but are worried about missing out on the cake excitement, you can always try some smörgåstårta, which translates as "sandwich cake", where bread and creamy sandwich filling are used to form layers. It is served cold in slices, just like a savoury cake.

Laura Andrews

3 Sing Snapsvisor In The Summer Sun

"Jag drar på semester nu, vi ses om en månad"
I'm going on holiday now, see you in a month

Summer in Sweden is beautiful and Stockholm is no exception. The evenings are long and the sun rises early in the morning, with over 18 hours of daylight on the longest days. The cloudless sky reflects in the water, turning the whole city a picturesque blue.

The start of April, when the restaurants open their outdoor serving, marks the start of spring, and although there is no guarantee the snow will have gone, everyone has a smile on their face. Even Swedes themselves will admit that they are the most open and friendly at this time of year. At the end of June, Swedes celebrate the most Swedish holiday of them all, midsummer. This is one of the most anticipated holidays of the year and usually an event for family and close friends, with maypole dancing and drinking songs (snapsvisor). It also marks the start of summer, with Swedes typically taking a month to six weeks off on summer holiday. Many Stockholmers leave the city and head for the peace and relaxation of the archipelago, to enjoy the summer in their summer houses. As a result, from midsummer until the beginning of August, the city can be relatively quiet and many shops and restaurants are closed, so it pays to plan ahead and check things are open before you set off.

>TOURIST

Don't let the prospect of some places being closed put you off visiting Stockholm in the summer though, it is still the capital city after all and there is always plenty to do and see. One of the highlights of summer is exploring the archipelago, which is much less accessible in winter when the water has frozen over.

4. Wrap Up Warm For Winter

"Det finns inget dåligt väder, bara dåliga kläder"
There's no such thing as bad weather, only the wrong clothes

If you ask a Swede when it's best to visit they will always say summer, however, Swedes are obsessed with sunshine and if you live in a place that doesn't get much snow, winter in Stockholm is magical. Daylight hours are a little on the short side (around 6 hours in December), but the city is filled with lights, as shops, restaurants and bars stand lanterns outside to welcome you in. At Christmas you will find Christmas tree branches on the ground across doorways, Christmas goats made of straw (julbock) in the windows and Christmas gnomes (tomte, a kind of Scandinavian Santa Claus) hiding in the corners. Also not to be forgotten is the Christmas buffet (julbord), which (unless you've been to Norway or Denmark) promises to be like no other buffet you've ever eaten and is served at many restaurants during the Christmas period. There are also several Christmas markets in Stockholm where you can buy traditional

Swedish foods and handcrafted items, which make excellent Christmas presents.

Although the authorities do a good job of clearing the snow, it can get slippery in the winter, so be sure to wear a good pair of shoes. Shoes with a soft rubber sole should do the trick. Stockholmers manage to keep stylish throughout the winter, so a wool coat and black boots will help you fit in with the crowd, although more practical outdoor brands such as Sweden's fashionable Fjällräven are also popular.

Heating in Sweden is cheap and buildings are well insulated so, while it's cold outside, it's usually warm inside. Layers of clothing are recommended otherwise you'll find yourself regretting that choice of thick wool jumper once you're indoors.

5. Decide Where To Stay

"Jag bor på Grand Hotel"
I am staying at the Grand Hotel

Situated across 14 islands, there's no escaping the water from the lake Mälaren, the third largest fresh water lake in Sweden, which surrounds the city before flowing into the Baltic Sea to the east. Discovering new places as you try to find a bridge to a neighbouring island is just part of Stockholm's charm.

>TOURIST

Stockholm is relatively small and has a good transport system. It is therefore possible to get across the centre in around half an hour meaning that, wherever you chose to stay, you can still easily access other parts of the city. Each island has its own feel, from the sophistication of Vasastan to the creative vibe of Södermalm; where you choose to stay is just a matter of taste and budget.

There are many high-end hotels in Stockholm, situated throughout the city centre, however there are also more affordable options, such as boat hostels moored at the edge of the lake Mälaren. If you're looking for centrally located accommodation with a city centre vibe then hotels around fashionable Östermalm and Kungsträdgården, or alternatively lively Martiatorget in Södermalm, are ideal.

However, if you want to avoid the city prices, accommodation slightly out of the centre is more affordable, while it's still easy to access all the central attractions using the metro (tunnelbana).

6. Get Into The City

"Var ligger Arlanda-Expressen?"
Which way is the Arlanda Express?

There are three airports in the vicinity of Stockholm, these are Arlanda, Bromma and Skavsta. All of these are serviced by airport busses (Flygbussarna), which run directly from the airport into the city centre, with several stops along the way. Tickets can be bought online or via the app (which are usually cheaper) or at the ticket machines in

Laura Andrews

the airport or near the bus stop. You can also buy tickets on board, although you will need to pay by card as cash is not accepted on public transport in Stockholm. The airport busses have luggage storage space, free wifi and you can charge your phone on route.

Arlanda airport is the largest of the three. The journey from Arlanda to Stockholm by bus takes around 45 minutes, however, there is also a train (the Arlanda Express), which can get you into Stockholm's Central Station in around 20 minutes. Tickets must be bought in advance of boarding, either online, via the app or at the train station. If you are pushed for time, the train is the best option, however the bus is cheaper and stops in several places around town, so may be more convenient depending on where you are staying.

Bromma is the closest airport to the city, taking around 20 minutes to central Stockholm by airport bus. Although the airport bus is most convenient, it is also possible to use Stockholm's public busses (run by SL), meaning you can save money if you are planning to buy an SL travelcard for getting around town anyway.

From Skavsta airport, the most straightforward way to get to Stockholm city centre is on the airport bus, which takes around 80 minutes.

If you would prefer to take a taxi there is usually a fixed price from the airport into town. As with most things in Stockholm, it is possible to pay the taxi fare by card, so no cash is required if you'd prefer to travel without it. Taxi can be a good value option if there's a group of you travelling together.

>TOURIST

7. Get Around Like A Local

"Jag vill köpa en sjudagarsbiljett, tack"
I would like to buy a seven-day ticket please

Stockholm has an excellent public transport system. The whole network is operated by one company (SL), meaning your SL ticket can be used on all forms of transport (except on some boats out to the archipelago). You must buy your ticket in advance before attempting to travel. Tickets can be purchased at metro (tunnelbana/t-bana) stations, many local newsagents such as 7-Eleven and Pressbyrån or at the Arlanda airport Visitor Centre. If you want to purchase a ticket to last you a few days, you will also need to get an SL Access Card to load the ticket on. You need to pay a small one-off fee for the card, but you can keep it for your next visit. You can also load the card with credit to pay for single use tickets, these are valid for 75 minutes, during which time you can travel as much as you like throughout the city. In addition to using the SL card, it is possible to buy single use tickets via SMS or through the SL app. Once you've bought your ticket, whatever the type, you just have to remember to touch in when you start your journey.

The metro runs quite late into the night and operates all night on Friday and Saturday. There are also night buses that run on the major routes throughout the week, making it easy to get home after a late night out.

Laura Andrews

Walking and cycling are also popular methods for getting around and, in my opinion, the best way to experience the city.

Aside from transporting you from A to B, Stockholm's underground metro is also a work of art, said to be the world's longest art exhibit. There is even a tour in English during the summer. Kungsträdgården, at the end of the blue line is my favourite. It has one of the most impressive designs and tells the history of the ground above.

8. Take In The History, Culture And Glamour Of Norrmalm And Östermalm

"Jag skulle vilja hyra ett par skridskor"
I would like to hire a pair of ice skates

In the northern part of the city lies Norrmalm (norr meaning north) and close by, to the north-east, is Östermalm (öst meaning east). Norrmalm feels like the real centre of the city, home to a wealth of restaurants, hotels, businesses and shops as well as T-Centralen, the central transport hub. If you walk from T-Centralen, up Kungsgatan (the king's street), you will reach Hötorget and a market square with fresh fruits, vegetables and flowers for sale. A short walk from here is the location where Swedish Prime Minister Olof Palme was assassinated in 1986, while walking home from the cinema with his wife. There is a plaque on the ground to mark the location, near to where Sveavägen meets Tunnelgatan/Olof Palmes Gata. I always look

>TOURIST

out for the plaque as I walk by as it seems strange that such a huge part of Stockholm's history can be so easily missed on a normal-looking shopping street.

In the southern part of Norrmalm there is a large park, Kungsträdgården (the king's garden). Here, in addition to the fountains and orderly flower beds, you will find many outdoor cafes. The park is also host to events throughout the year, including concerts and festivals of culture, food and arts. In the summer the cherry blossoms make a beautiful sight, lining the pathways the full length of the park. In the winter there is an outdoor ice-skating rink, but for me the best part is the coffee hut that comes with it. Here you can buy a hotdog, which you then cook yourself over the open fire. There's nothing that says winter more than wrapping up warm, huddling around a fire and cooking hotdogs and drinking coffee.

Just a short walk to the east of Norrmalm is Östermalm, which is known as the wealthy part of town, with high housing prices and designer shops. It is also host to many upmarket restaurants and is the place to go for those looking for a more glamorous nightlife.

Laura Andrews

9. Find A Restaurant To Suit Your Taste On Rörstrandgatan

"Äter bör man, annars dör man"
One should eat, otherwise one will die

Rörstrandgatan in Vasastan is the place to go if you're hungry but not quite sure what type of restaurant to choose or you haven't got a reservation, as due to the sheer volume of restaurants it's usually possible to find a vacant table. Here you will find Indian, Japanese, Persian, Swedish, French and burger restaurants (Swedes love burgers) as well as a Scottish pub. Indian Garden (which also has several other restaurants around the city) offers arguably some of the best Indian food in Stockholm, while Tehran Grill is recommended for real authentic Persian cuisine.

In the summer the street is pedestrianised and the restaurants take over with their massive outdoor seating areas. This makes it extremely popular as no Swede wants to sit indoors during the summer, regardless of the temperature. Restaurants will pull out large piles of blankets at a moment's notice if there is even a hint of a chill in the air and the locals will wrap themselves up and leave their sunglasses on to the bitter end. In the evenings it's a very popular area with Stockholmers coming for a drink and dinner after work. A go-to place when deciding on a laid back or uncharacteristically spontaneous evening out.

>TOURIST

10. Enjoy Cocktails In The Courtyard In Stureplan

"Kan du rekommenderar en god cocktail?"
Can you recommend a good cocktail?

Stureplan is located in posh Östermalm and the nightlife reflects this. This is where you go if you want to get dressed up and mingle with the beautiful people of Stockholm.

The easy thing about Stureplan is that it is a small area, alive with bars and clubs, meaning you can just set off in that direction and see where the evening takes you. Of course, that kind of spontaneity isn't very Swedish, but if you go out early enough in the evening (before 10 pm on a weekend - things start to liven up around 11pm) you won't need to worry that you didn't book yourself on that guest list several weeks ago.

As with many places in Stockholm, mixing the outside with the inside is popular for bars around Stureplan. This is particularly important in the summer, when no self-respecting Stockholmer would dream of going to a venue without an outside area. Grand Escalier has a restaurant and lounge area but, most importantly, an inner courtyard with a bar, open all year round. It's an excellent place to grab a cocktail or two and enjoy the surroundings. If you're looking for somewhere to dance, but aren't ready to head inside yet, you can make

Laura Andrews

your way to Nosh and Chow. On the second floor they have several bars and an inner courtyard, including a fireplace next to the DJ booth.

11. Lounge Around At Lydmar Hotel

"Låt oss softa med en kopp kaffe"
Let's just chill with a cup of coffee

Lydmar Hotel on Södra Blasieholmshamnen in Norrmalm has great views, great décor and great coffee. The bar and dining room is one and the same or there are large comfy armchairs and sofas in the lobby. The stylish, colourful interior and mix of guests make for pleasant surroundings, and on Sunday afternoons there is often a DJ playing some chilled out Sunday tunes. It is conveniently located close to many of Stockholm's main tourist attractions, so is the perfect place to come to relax for a while after a busy day sightseeing. They also serve excellent coffee, for a bit of a pick me up.

If it's a sunny day, you will find the Stockholmers lined up on the patio at the front of the hotel, faces to the sun, a drink in hand. The patio is opposite the water and is a nice place for people and boat watching. If you prefer something a bit more secluded, there is also a roof-top terrace on the second floor, styled as a French garden, which is open from May to September. Lydmar Hotel also holds events and club nights; these can be found on the events calendar on their website.

>TOURIST

12. Dare To Take A Ghost Walk Through The Old Town

"Oj! Jag tror att jag såg ett spöke!"
Oh! I think I saw a ghost!

Gamla Stan or the "Old Town" is, as its name suggests, the oldest part of Stockholm, founded in 1252. The island is a popular place with tourists, but is still worth a visit to see the narrow, cobbled streets and well-preserved medieval buildings. It's also a good opportunity to pick up any souvenirs in its touristy yet quirky shops. Nestled deep in the centre of Gamla Stan is the old town square, which holds a Christmas market throughout December. Even if you're not in the shopping mood, the Christmas market is a nice place to come to get into the Christmassy spirit with some glögg and lussekatter (see chapter 2 on fika!). Remember to also look out for the tiny market stall hidden inside the well.

One fun way to learn about the history of Gamla Stan is by taking a Ghost Walk tour. Although, if you like the idea of it being spooky, you might want to get all your warmest clothes on and join a tour in the winter when the evenings are dark.

While visiting Gamla Stan, you should take a short detour to Riddarholmen, an island right beside Gamla Stan. Aside from the beautiful old buildings there is also Riddarholm Church

Laura Andrews

(Riddarholmskyrka), which is one of Stockholm's oldest buildings and traditionally the final resting place for Swedish monarchs.

13. Enjoy A Cosy Meal At Stockholms Gastabud

"Jag vill ha toast skagen och köttbullar, tack"
I will have prawns on toast and meatballs please

If you want some good Swedish food in a friendly, laid-back environment then look no further than Stockholms Gastabud. Located on Österlånggatan 7 in Gamla Stan, you could easily walk by this unassuming but charming restaurant. Here they serve a range of Swedish dishes in a homely environment. Its small size and decor make it a particularly cosy place to spend a winter afternoon or evening.

Although it can be busy and you may have to wait for a table, don't let that put you off, just relax in the small bar area with a drink while you wait. Once seated, despite its size and no lack of demand for tables, you never feel rushed and the staff are very friendly. The portions are good and the prices are reasonable. All in all Stockholms Gastabud gives you everything you could ever want from a Swedish restaurant experience (including meatballs and toast skagen, the best of Swedish foods) and I always take my friends and family there.

>TOURIST

14. Climb The Town Hall Tower

"Oj, vad många trappor!"
Oh, what a lot of stairs!

Kungsholmen lies in the western part of central Stockholm and is a more residential area, although not lacking in restaurants and shops. There is a footpath that goes around the whole of the island and is a popular walking, running and cycling route for locals, with a couple of outdoor gyms included along the way if you're feeling particularly active. The whole path is around 10 km long, however it's possible to just walk parts of it as well.

It is Kunghsolmen where you will find the City Hall (Stadshuset). You can take a guided tour through the whole building, or just take a trip up to the top of the tower, from where you'll see amazing aerial views of Gamla Stan, as well as the rest of the city. However, if you don't feel like climbing all those stairs you can still enjoy a beautiful view across the water to Gamla Stan and Södermalm. There's nothing quite as relaxing as sitting on the steps, with the water lapping by your feet, watching the ferries and canoeists go by. This is also the best place to get a classic Stockholm photo, looking across the water at the iconic cast iron spire of Riddarholm church.

Laura Andrews

15. Relax By The Lake At Norr Mälarstrand

"Detta är nog min favoritplats"
This might be one of my favourite places

Norr Mälarstrand lies on the south side of Kungsholmen and makes up part of the footpath that you can walk all the way around the island. The path follows the northern side of the lake Mälaren, hence the name Norr Mälarstrand (northern shore of lake Mälaren). While the whole path around the island is lovely to walk along, this specific section, which runs from Rålambhovs park down to the City Hall, is very popular among locals for both its beauty and a couple of great places to stop for refreshments in the summer.

From the tree-lined path, which runs along the edge of the water, you can see stunning views of Södermalm and the Western Bridge (Västerbron). Starting from Rålambshovs Park, the first place you come to is Mälarpaviljongen, a pavilion located in a garden on a floating dock on the lake, and one of the best summer locations in Stockholm. This outdoor, floating cafe/bar/garden-centre hybrid serves food, fika and drinks, in a setting of beautiful plants and flowers, and you can also pick up something for your garden while you're there.

As you walk towards the City Hall, you emerge from the trees and, in summer, can usually enjoy an ice cream from the waterside ice cream stand. There are a small handful of restaurants and bars along

>TOURIST

the water here in the summer, some of them also on floating docks in the lake. However, Orangeriet is open all year round and provides food, drinks and beautiful décor. In the summer there is a roof top terrace where you can enjoy the sun and the lake views, while in the winter you can cosy up on one of the sofas by the fire inside and look out over the snow covered hills of Södermalm and the frozen water of lake Mälaren.

16. Hang Out At Hornsbergstrand

"Ska vi ta en strand promenad?"
Shall we take a walk by the water?

Hornsbergstrand lies on the northern edge of Kungsholmen and also forms part of the footpath that runs around the whole island. It is largely a residential area with several restaurants, however it also has the most fantastic view out across the water. As it is slightly further out from the very centre of the city, Hornsberg strand is a calmer place to relax and enjoy the view, although, like every sunny spot in Stockholm, it can be busier on hot days as everyone comes out to enjoy the weather.

In contrast to the rest of central Stockholm, Hornsberg Strand is a modern environment. There is a place to swim as well as a decked area, popular with sunbathers on warm days. Here you can walk along the water or simply sit and look out to the islands on the other side.

Laura Andrews

While it is a great sunny spot in the summer, I also find it to be very beautiful on cold and wet days when there's no one around.

There are several restaurants and cafes that line the waterfront at Hornsberg Strand, however it is Piren that has the best location. It stands on a pier in the water and has glass walls, meaning you can have a view of the water whether sitting inside or out, summer or winter.

17. Enjoy The Summer Outdoors At Solstugan

"Här skiner alltid solen"
"Here the sun is always shining"

Solstugan (translated as the sun cottage/cabin) sits on top of the cliffs in Fredhäll, Kungsholmen (at Snoilskyvägen 37) and therefore has a fantastic view over the water. Set back from the road and surrounded by trees, even walking down the small path to Solstugan feels like an exciting little adventure. This is a place you can always rely on in summer as, come rain or shine, you are guaranteed to be able to sit outside and enjoy the view thanks to outdoor heaters and a roof that can be pulled over at short notice. They also always save places for drop-in guests, so it's ideal if you're feeling a little more spontaneous.

>TOURIST

There is always a laid-back, friendly atmosphere, and you can eat lunch or dinner, as well as just relax with a drink. In addition to the food and drink, there is sometimes live music from bands and DJs on the upper deck, however you can still enjoy a calmer atmosphere on the lower deck if you want something a little quieter.

As the ultimate summer hang out, Solstugan is only open from April to early September.

18. Challenge Your Friends At Boulebar And Ugglan

"Tio spänn på att jag kommer vinna"
I bet ten bucks that I will win

Boules and shuffle board are particularly popular ways to while away and evening or afternoon for Stockholmers. There are several places in the city where you can play games while you have a drink with your friends, but Boulebar and Ugglan are, in my opinion, two of the best.

If you're not very competitive and just want to relax outdoors in the park and play some boules, then Boulebar in Rålambshov park is a great place to go. Rålambshov park itself is situated on Kungsholmen and is a large space for all kinds of activities, such as skateboarding, outdoor workouts and volleyball as well as just relaxing and taking a walk. Boulebar is on the east side of the park, near the lake. They offer

Laura Andrews

French inspired food and drinks including a large range of pastis and we are told that, according to French boules tradition, the winner always buys a round. You can drop by to play anytime, or alternatively book your boule time in advance. Boulebar in Rålambshov park is only open during the summer, however they have other indoor locations, which are open all year round.

If you're feeling super competitive and want more than boules, or you're just really bad at boules, then you can drop by Ugglan at Nytorget on Södermalm. Advertised as a recreation centre for adults, Ugglan has lots of different games including the classic shuffleboard and boules, but also "rundpingis", which essentially involves a large group of people running around a table tennis table and trying to keep the ball moving, as well as air hockey, arcade games and more. They also serve food and have a bar.

19. Play It Cool In Södermalm

"Så många kyrkor och hipsters har jag aldrig sett"
I've never seen so many churches and hipsters

Södermalm (locally known as just Söder, meaning "south") is an island in the southern part of central Stockholm. Södermalm was originally a working class area, however with the expansion of the city it increasingly became more desirable to live and spend time there. Today Söder is a firmly fashionable place to be, known for its

>TOURIST

alternative culture and stereotyped as being a cool, hipster area with a more relaxed feel than its northern counterparts. You can drop by one of the many second-hand shops in the area to get a Söder-style hipster look of your own.

Södermalm is characterised by its blend of old and new, with 18th century houses meeting 21st century buildings. It is also home to quite a few churches. The island was originally very rocky, however thanks to Alfred Nobel inventing dynamite in the neighbouring area, it was possible to blast through the rock and create new areas of the city. This gives Södermalm a unique feeling. With some buildings built into the rocks it feels like the city is intertwined with the nature and is a really quirky feature. The rocky terrain also means that much of wandering around Södermalm involves walking up hill, although it is worth the effort for the views, of which there are many, with the best viewpoints all being favourite hang outs for the island's locals. Most places are easily accessible by public footpath, although it can be slippery in winter.

Laura Andrews

20. Stroll Through Södermalm

"Titta! En häst gömmer sig där!"
Look! There is a horse hiding there!

One of my favourite things to do in Stockholm is to just walk around and I always recommend it as the best way to take in the city's atmosphere. In the quiet backstreets of Södermalm, you can follow Katarina Bangata. The tree-lined footpath goes all the way from Medborgarplatsen down to water on the south side of the island and is a great way of experiencing the charm of Södermalm without having to worry about getting lost; just follow the path and let your mind wander as you look at the scenery. If you enjoy stumbling across unexpected statues, start the walk in Fatburs park (Fatbursparken), where you may be able to find the Secret Horses hiding under one of the archways. After that follow Katarina Bangata and keep your eye out for the sporadic sculptures on the way, each with their own history. Along the route you will pass through Greta Garbo's Square (Greta Garbo's Torg) and you will also be able to see a glimpse of one of Stockholm's many churches, Sofiakyrka.

Once you get to the end of the path you reach the Winter Toll (Vintertullen), named as such because of the toll gates that were once situated around Stockholm. Tolls were implemented in 1622 to collect duties on all edible, wearable and consumable goods that were brought into the city to be sold. At this time a high fence was built all around the city to prevent anyone from importing goods without paying the fees, with toll gates set up at various places. You will notice several place names in Stockholm which end in "tull" (such as Hornstull and Skanstull) where toll gates used to be. However, in winter, when traders used to bring their produce over the frozen lake, special winter toll gates were erected. At Vintertullen you will also find a park overlooking the water, which is a nice place to sit and relax on a warm day.

21. Continue The Stroll Through Södermalm

"Lite frisk luft har ingen dött av"
A bit of fresh air never killed anyone

If you continue from Vintertullen, you can walk along the south shore of Södermalm, from Eriksdalsbadet (Sweden's national swimming arena) all the way to Tanto (a large outdoor park). This walk gives you a real out-of-town feeling, despite still being in the centre of Stockholm. On route you will pass boats, outdoor gyms and picturesque allotments with their colourfully painted huts, giving a real feeling for how Stockholmers like to spend their free time. There is even a floating sauna in the lake. The sauna is run by members and does offer some public drop-in times, however these are typically advertised in their Facebook group (in Swedish) and payment is by swish (which requires a Swedish bank account), so best to drag a swede along with you if you're planning a trip.

Laura Andrews

In the summer you'll find pop-up food trucks and there is even a beach, which is a popular place for families to spend a sunny afternoon. If you don't feel brave enough to swim in the lake, you can take advantage of the outdoor pool at Eriksdalsbadet where you can also enjoy waterslides in the water palace.

22. Dinner And A Movie At Bio Rio

"Vilken film vill du se?"
Which film do you want to see?

Situated by the water at Hornstulls strand 3 on Södermalm is arthouse cinema Bio Rio, a single screen cinema from the 1940s, and it retains its old-world feeling well. The cinema shows films from all around the world, both indie and Hollywood blockbusters. Films in Sweden are subtitled rather than dubbed (with the exception of children's films), meaning you'll be able to watch the film in its original language, with Swedish subtitles. So no need to worry if your Swedish isn't quite up to scratch.

Dinner and a movie has never been easier as Bio Rio serves its own meals, and the food is really good. If you want to make a long evening of it, you can book a table at Bistro Rio. Here they serve French-inspired vegetarian food, made from local produce and range of wines and beers.

>TOURIST

If you're a bit more pressed for time but don't want to miss out on dinner or the film then you can do both in the lounge area situated at the back of the cinema. This feels like such a luxury as you can enjoy being served a meal, or even just snacks and drinks, while you watch the film. It's a far cry from the experience you get in modern day cinemas. You need to book in advance if you wish to eat in the cinema and food needs to be ordered 30 minutes before the start of the film.

23. Brunch Or More At Kvarnen

"Vilken härlig frunch buffé!"
What a lovely brunch buffet!

Brunch is a popular weekend activity in Stockholm, although the concept of it being a combination of breakfast and lunch seems lost on the Swedes, with most brunches starting at midday, making it more of a lunch. Regardless, it's still an excellent way to while away a lazy afternoon. One of the best weekend brunch places is Kvarnen. Located near Medborgarplatsen on Södermalm, it has been around since 1908 and is one of Stockholm's oldest beer halls, giving the place a very distinctive character. For brunch, a huge buffet of delicious hot and cold Swedish foods is served; make sure you are hungry when you arrive. There are some times of year when brunch is not available and the rest of the time it's very popular, so it's best to book in advance.

Laura Andrews

If you have already filled your weekend with brunches, but want to experience Kvarnen, you can also enjoy a dinner of traditional Swedish food in their restaurant. Or better yet, take in the lively and friendly atmosphere in the bar during the evenings. If you're the type of person who likes to end their night on the dance floor, there is a small night club in the basement. Aside from the delicious food, Kvarnen just feels like a really cool place to be, with all the buzz of a popular local bar. Except for the club. That's really not a cool place to be, but it's a perfect place to just have fun and dance with friends.

24. Check Out A Photography Exhibition At Fotografiska

"Vilken vacker utställning!"
What a beautiful exhibition!

If you want a brunch with a sprinkling of culture then there is Fotografiska. Located by the water in the north of Södermalm and housed in a stylish industrial building from the early 1900s, Fotografiska exhibits photographers from all around the world and with several exhibitions running at once, there is usually something to peak your interest.

On the top floor you can find a cafe, restaurant and bar with stunning views over the water. The food on offer is usually seasonal, with a focus on vegetables, making it vegetarian and vegan friendly,

>TOURIST

although there are also meat and fish options available. Brunch is available on the weekends and is my favourite way to enjoy Fotografiska as, for a fixed price, you get entrance to the museum as well as the brunch buffet. There is a wide range of hot and cold dishes, but don't overlook the dessert table as it's one of the best parts. Be sure to book a few weeks in advance as it is very popular. Alternatively you can just pop in to the cafe for a fika and to enjoy the scenery after taking a look at the photography exhibitions. In the evenings there are often DJs and other events too.

25. Eat Vegetarian Food With A View At Hermans

"Jag aldrig ätit så här god vegetarisk mat"
I never thought vegetarian food could be so good

Vegetarianism, or at least part-time vegetarianism, is becoming increasingly popular in Stockholm, as if Swedes could get any more health and/or environmentally conscious. As such, there is a wealth of really good (and popular) vegetarian restaurants. One of which, famous not only for its vegetarian and vegan food, but also for the fabulous view is Hermans. Located on Fjällgatan 23B on Södermalm, Hermans sits on top of a hill overlooking the water and has a large outdoor space in the summer. Inside, it is simple and casual, but whether you're a vegetarian or not, the food at Hermans never ceases to pleasantly surprise in both variety and taste. You pay a flat fee for an all-you-can-eat buffet comprising of hot and cold dishes, soup, salads, sauces and home-made breads. They also have a large range of vegan desserts and fika available, which you pay for separately. These are also very tasty, so be sure to save room.

If visiting Stockholm over the Christmas period, make sure you try out Herman's Christmas buffet (julbord). If you were at all put off from a regular julbord by the bread dipped in ham broth, the boiled white fish and the range of pickled herring, then Hermans vegetarian julbord may well be the right alternative for you.

26. Walk In History's Footsteps Down Fjällgatan

"Det är som att resa tillbaka i tiden"
It's like going back in time

If you happen to be in the area (which of course you will be to visit Hermans and Fotografiska) then take a few minutes to walk down Fjällgatan and admire both the view and the old houses, some of which date back to the 1700s. Instead of the large, sometimes imposing buildings that characterise other areas of the city, these houses are somewhat smaller and many are made of wood, painted different colours, with wooden shutters at the windows. Walking down Fjällgatan gives you a real sense of what Stockholm once would have been like.

>TOURIST

As well as the quaint, old buildings, Fjällgatan offers yet another stunning panoramic view of northern Stockholm. From here you can watch the rollercoaster rides in Gröna Lund and the giant cruise ships that moor in Södermalm before heading out to the Baltic Sea.

Of course, no view point would be complete without a place to buy fika, and Fjällgatan has its own coffee hut, which has been there since 1968 and serves coffee, cakes and ice cream.

27. Watch The Sun Set Over The City At Mossebacketerassen

"Oj, vilken fin utsikt!"
Wow, what a great view!

Mosebacketerrassen lies just off Mosebacke Square in Södermalm and here you suddenly stumble across a breath-taking view of Stockholm, looking towards the north of the city including Gamla Stan and Djurgården. In addition to the wonderful view, the spacious terrace is home to several bars, so you can stop here, grab a drink, sit on the wooden benches and soak up the atmosphere. There is also a small stage, where Swedish bands will occasionally play live, creating a really upbeat. fun and lively environment.

The views from Mossebacketerrassen are particularly beautiful around the height of summer, when the evenings are long and you can

Laura Andrews

watch the sun set slowly over the rooftops. It is the kind of place that creates moments that remind you how privileged you are to be able to spend an evening relaxing with such incredible surroundings.

Being an outdoor venue, the bars at Mossebacketerassen are only open during the summer, however the view can be enjoyed all year round and while some people find Stockholm's grey and white winter scenery somewhat bleak, I have always found it dramatic and very photo worthy.

28. Eat Traditional Swedish Food At Pelikan

"Smaklig målitd!"
Enjoy your meal!

Another Swedish restaurant with a long history of serving great food, Pelikan, can be found on Blekingegatan 40 on Södermalm. The name Pelikan dates back to the 17th century and while the location and owners have changed a few times over the years, the restaurant has always been known for its good food. The high ceilings and vintage decor consisting of dark wood panelling and a tiled floor make it easy to get a sense of history when entering the place, it doesn't feel like just any old restaurant, but rather more old-world Stockholm.

The chefs at Pelikan take the art of real traditional Swedish food seriously so don't expect to find a burger here. While, at a glance, the

>TOURIST

menu may appear a bit strange it won't be long before you're indulging yourself with toast skagen (prawns on toast), reindeer and västerbotten pie (traditional cheese pie). However if you're feeling less adventurous, the classic Swedish dish of meatballs and mashed potatoes with lingonberry jam, is an excellent choice. They also have a large selection of different types of aquavit, should you dare to try the traditional Scandinavian drink. Why not even prepare a drinking song (snapsvisor) in advance to fully immerse yourself in Swedish culture?

29. Party Under The Bridge

"Ska vi mingla i baren?"
Should we go and mingle in the bar?

If you're the kind of person who is cool enough to party under a bridge, then this is the place for you. Located under the Skanstull bridge in Södermalm (Hammarby Slussväg 2), you will find a club in winter and a mini festival in summer.

Trädgården is the outdoor summer club with a festival vibe. Aside from the several bar areas, serving a range of drinks and with different DJs, you can also play ping pong, grab a bite to eat or, proper festival style, charge your mobile phone at the charging station. There is really no reason to ever leave. As much of the club is outside, remember to take a jacket with you to fend off any chills once the sun goes down (although it will be back up again very shortly). Get there early evening for free entrance and to enjoy a more laid-back feeling and the opportunity to explore the different areas before it gets busy.

When it's finally too cold and dark to happily hang out under the bridge, it's time to take it inside to winter club Under Bron (Under The Bridge), where you will find a variety of international DJs playing across several bars. Under Bron is open until 5am, giving you plenty of time to gain the full experience, although queues to get in can be really long if you arrive later in the evening (around midnight).

30. Climb Skinnarvik Mountain

"Behöver jag klättringutrustning? – Nej, bara fika"
Do I need climbing equipment? – No, just fika

Less of a climb and more of a very short, casual uphill walk, Skinnarvik mountain (Skinnarviksberg) is Stockholm's highest natural viewpoint and can be found on rocky Södermalm. From the top you can see the whole of northern Stockholm, all the way from the Western Bridge to Kaknäs Tower in the east. Skinnarvik mountain is a popular place for locals to come for a picnic or just to enjoy the long summer evenings. In the winter, if the northern lights are strong enough to be visible in Stockholm (this happens very rarely), then this is one of the best places you will have a chance of seeing them, with its uninhibited view of the northern sky.

>TOURIST

Walking down from the mountain, you will come across Old Lundagatan (Gamla Lundagatan), where workers and poor people previously lived when the area was surrounded by tobacco factories, textile mills and a brewery (Munchenbryggeriet - the impressive building is today used for conferences and concerts). Some of the original houses, made from stone and wood in the 1700s still stand, in fact, there are several old houses and buildings in the area, making it a really interesting place to just amble around and have a look.

Just a short walk further and you will come across Montseliusvägen, a pathway that meanders along the cliff side, through trees and passed old houses. There are stunning views of Riddarholmen and the Town Hall as well as across the city. You can also stop off and relax at Ivar Los Park on the way, with its charmingly Swedish playground for children and grassy spaces for adults to relax.

31. Go Vegan With Lunch At Mahalo

"Vänta! Jag måste ta en bild"
Wait, I need to take a picture

Once you've got a taste for all things vegetarian, you can be assured to find somewhere to eat on Hornsgatan, Södermalm. However, why not step it up a notch and go vegan at lively cafe Mahalo, located at Hornsgatan 61. One look at any of the stunningly colourful, Instagram-ready dishes will wash away any doubts you may ever have had about wanting to try vegan food and leave you reaching for your camera.

As well as the colourful dishes, they also serve a range of juices, smoothies, shots and milkshakes to help you boost your daily fruit and veggie intake.

The interior is casual, but bright and upbeat. It can get busy around lunchtimes and at the weekends, so be prepared to queue a little, but your patience will be rewarded.

32. Keep An Eye Out For Benny From ABBA At Hotel Rival

"Är det Benny som äger det här hotellet?"
Is it Benny who owns this hotel?

Hotel Rival is all your needs in one place, with a hotel, bar, bistro and café, located at Mariatorget in Södermalm. It is owned by Benny Andersson of ABBA fame and so if you don't fancy making that trip to the ABBA museum but still want some ABBA anecdotes to take back home, this is the place to come. On the other hand, if you're a really big ABBA fan then be sure to check out the song "2nd Best to None", written by Benny and Björn specially for Hotel Rival and recorded by the hotel staff.

>TOURIST

Part of the building is from the 1930s and so, following this theme, the cocktail bar is art-deco inspired and serves cocktails appropriate for that time, giving you the whole 1930s experience. The DJs at the weekend give this bar a modern twist and make it a popular place for a night out. Remember to dress up for the occasion!

If none of the above appeals, you can always make sure you get your fika quota at Cafe Rival, which serves a large range of cakes along with different coffees and teas.

33. EAT BREAKFAST AT BAZZAR

"Morgonstund har guld i mun"
Literally translates as "morning time has gold in mouth"
i.e. the early bird catches the worm

If you thought you couldn't get excited about another Swedish breakfast of breads and cheeses, or you simply can't get enough, Bazzar is the perfect place to visit. Located in a quiet corner of Södermalm (Bondegatan 59), this cafe is guaranteed to inspire you to bring a bit of Swedish culture back home with you and start having a Swedish-style breakfast every morning. On top of the great food, nothing gives you a more positive feeling than strolling through the quiet Södermalm streets on a bright morning as you make your way there.

Laura Andrews

Once you've worked up an appetite with a morning walk, you can enjoy a range of freshly-baked breads and cheeses and meats all so beautifully presented you will once again be reaching for your camera. If you can't possibly decide between all the different options, why not go for a breakfast plate where you can try a bit of everything with the addition of yoghurt, an egg and a salad. It goes without saying that you can also enjoy delicious juices and coffee. The interior is bright and colourful and the friendly, welcoming staff give the place a relaxed atmosphere. The perfect place to start your day before heading out to explore the city.

Just around the corner is Sofia church and Vitabergs park, which are beautiful to look at and recommended for walking off your large breakfast.

34. Escape The City On The Prison Island

"Det är skönt att vi bara besöka fängelset!"
It's nice that we are only visiting the prison!

Långholmen is an island situated between Södermalm and Kungsholmen and is the perfect place to escape the noise and bustle. However the fact that Stockholmers are able to enjoy this inner-city oasis today is all down to the island's slightly darker history.

>TOURIST

From the 1720s until 1975 Långholmen was home to a prison. The island was originally rocky and bare, however the prisoners were ordered to cover large areas of the island with mud from the surrounding lake and plant nearly 3000 trees. Further work was carried out in the 20th century to create paths and some structure, creating the Långholmen that can be seen today. Following its closure, the prison has been turned into a hotel, hostel and a prison museum. The hostel provides comparatively cheap and quirky accommodation right in the centre of Stockholm and you could combine it with a stay in a boat hostel for a truly memorable, but more affordable holiday.

In 1993 a fighter plane, which was involved in an air display, crashed on the island. Luckily only one spectator was injured and the pilot safely ejected, however there is now a sculpture at the site of the crash.

Today Långholmen is popular for casual walks, with beautiful views of Kungsholmen across the water. It is an excellent location for picnics and paddling in the lake by some of its beachy areas. The island also features an open-air theatre.

Laura Andrews

35. Walk Around Djurgården

"Vilken typ av blommar är detta?"
What type of flowers are these?

Djurgården is an island in the eastern part of central Stockholm. Here you will find some of the main tourist attractions, such as the Vasa museum, the Nordic Museum (Nordiska museet) and the ABBA museum, which are all essential to visit as you will be asked countless times by tourists and locals alike if you have visited them yet. Additionally, located on the island there is the Gröna Lund theme park and Skansen open-air museum. The island can be reached easily by walking from central Stockholm, or by tram, with some old-fashioned trams still running the route if you want that nostalgia feeling. If you don't have time to go out to the archipelago, but don't want to miss out on a boat trip, you can also access Djurgården via a very short ferry ride, for which your SL ticket is valid. Saving your walking legs on route to Djurgården is a good idea as the island itself is great fun to walk around, but quite large. One particular highlight is Rosendahl palace (slott) and garden (trädgård), but mostly the garden, which lies right next to the palace, in case you decide to venture to both. Fruits and vegetables are grown in the garden and it also has a rose garden and orchard.

Once you've been inspired by the plants around the garden you can make your way to the shop and pick up some of your own gardening

>TOURIST

supplies, or maybe a gift to take back home. However, if gardening really isn't your thing, you can head straight to the cafe and enjoy some lunch or just a fika. Even if you aren't the type of person who would usually visit a garden, Rosendahl garden is very charming and who doesn't enjoy sitting in an orchard in the sunshine, enjoying life with a cold drink or a cinnamon bun in their hand?

36. Get Familiar With Nordic Culture And Wildlife At Skansen

"Titta på björnen!"
Look at the bear!

Skansen is the world's oldest open-air museum and although it can get quite busy, it is fun to go, with or without children and you get a different experience every time, depending on the season. At Skansen you can learn what life used to be like for Swedes by seeing the buildings they lived in and how they worked. Just remember to get some traditional, home-made fika from the old bakery. Visitors can also learn about the Sami, who live in the north of Sweden, through taking a look at the Sami camp, which even includes a herd of reindeer.

In addition to the reindeer, Skansen offers a chance to see some other Nordic animals, including bears, wolves, lynxes, wolverines, moose and wild boar, among others. If you go during the winter, however, the bears will be hibernating and you won't be able to see them. There is also a children's section, where you can get up close to some of the more cuddly animals (regardless of whether you actually have children or not!). I highly recommend dropping by the baby goats.

Skansen has an aquarium, for which an extra admission is charged, however it is completely worth it as you get access not only to the aquarium but also the World of Monkeys, which is extremely fun.

There are always events going on at Skansen throughout the year, showing how the way of life changed with the seasons. The best festivities, in my opinion, are at Christmas when there is dancing around the Christmas tree in the town square.

Skansen is also home to "Allsång på Skansen" (translated as sing-along at Skansen), a popular weekly TV programme which airs throughout the summer. Here the audience sings along to well-known Swedish songs played live by popular Swedish musicians. If you really want to immerse yourself in Swedish culture, this is the place to be on a Tuesday night, along with seemingly the whole of Stockholm.

>TOURIST

37. Ride A Rollercoaster To Live Music At Gröna Lund

"Det här är mitt favoritband!"
They are my favourite band

Gröna Lund is a theme park located on Djurgården and is easily accessible by tram, bus and ferry. It is Sweden's oldest amusement park and has everything you would expect, such as rollercoasters, a haunted house and the chance to win giant bars of chocolate. It also has several restaurants cafes and bars.

One of the most loved things by locals about Gröna Lund is its summer concerts. Every year the venue hosts loads of concerts from May to September, with both Swedish and international music acts. Huge names such as Elton John, Bob Marley and Jimi Hendrix have all played in the past and every year you can be sure there will be a wide range of musical genres hitting the stage. You can get access to Gröna Lund and all the concerts simply by buying the very reasonably priced Green Card from the Gröna Lund ticket office. As a result, the whole of Stockholm owns a Green Card and, as the venue has a limited capacity, if you want to get in to see a popular artist, you need to arrive plenty early and be prepared to queue.

Laura Andrews

38. Be Overwhelmed By Cake At Kaknäs Tower

"Vill du dela?"
Do you want to share?

The Kaknäs tower (Kaknästornet) is a TV tower located in the north eastern part of Stockholm in Gärdet. At 155 metres high it has amazing views over Stockholm and you can watch the tiny horses in the near-by field and the footballers playing on a pitch that looks so small you can mistake it for a tennis court. It is also a great place for watching boats starting to make their journey out into the archipelago as well as those which are returning, something that is actually strangely mesmerising.

At the top of the tower there is a viewing platform, cafe and a restaurant. If you have a restaurant booking you don't need to pay to go up the tower, otherwise there is a fee per person. At the bottom of the tower there is a quite large gift shop, that usually has some interesting things.

If you can't decide between the restaurant and the cafe, I would strongly recommend the cafe. Aside from stunning views, the cafe has a wide range of options to compliment your fika. I suggest going with a few dessert-loving friends so you can grab a handful and share, because once you see the cake selection, your eyes will become bigger than your stomach and you won't know what to choose.

>TOURIST

39. See Where Nobel Experimented With Dynamite

"I Stockholm finns naturen alltid nära"
In Stockholm, the nature is always nearby

Vinterviken is an area to the west of central Stockholm and, if you're interested in Alfred Nobel, but don't fancy the Nobel museum, then Vinterviken is for you. Nobel bought the whole area following the death of his brother and several others in an explosion while experimenting with nitroglycerin. Vinterviken, at the time, was outside of the city and surrounded by cliffs, making it a safer location for his work. He built his factory here, producing dynamite until 1921.

Stockholm City now owns Vinterviken and has turned it into a recreational area for people to come and enjoy the nature. There is a restaurant and cafe, while one of Nobel's buildings has been turned into a banqueting hall. There are many cultural events held in Vinterviken, including live music and theatre and there are markets held three times a year where you can buy plants and produce, depending on the season.

Vinterviken is also a popular place to gather and celebrate traditional Swedish holidays such as midsummer, making it an excellent choice if you're visiting Stockholm during the holidays, but don't know anyone local to celebrate with. However, even if there are

Laura Andrews

no events on, Vinterviken is beautiful to simply take a walk around, any time of year.

40. Go Hiking In Tyresta National Park

"Har du packat smörgåsar och fika?"
Have you packed the sandwiches and the fika?

Sweden is covered in trees and adventures in the countryside are an important part of Swedish culture, so no trip would be complete without getting out and experiencing what it's like to walk through the middle of a forest. In Sweden everyone has a right to enjoy the countryside. This is called "allemansrätten" meaning "the freedom to roam," but also includes being allowed to pick berries and mushrooms as well as set up camp for an evening. However, with this freedom comes responsibility, so it is important to make sure you don't do anything to disturb the nature. As they say, "leave nothing but footprints, take nothing but photos".

A short journey outside of central Stockholm will get you to Tyresta National Park and Nature Reserve. You can reach it by bus from Gullmarsplan, just south of Södermalm, and the whole journey is covered by your SL ticket. There are many kilometres of hiking trails in the park, so finding somewhere to walk dependent on the time you want to spend and your ability shouldn't be a problem. There is also an information centre where you can find out more about the wildlife and

>TOURIST

get some help if you want to go camping and are unsure about the rules.

41. Experience Life In The Archipelago

"Med solkräm och badkläder är vi redo"
We've got sun cream and swimwear, now we're ready

There are nearly 30,000 islands, islets and rocks in Stockholm's archipelago. Many are inaccessible without your own boat, but there's still plenty of places that can be reached by public transport or boat taxi. Heading out to any of the islands during July and August provides a real insight into how Stockholmers spend their summer.

A popular island to visit in the summer is Utö. Situated in the far south of the archipelago, it takes several hours to reach by public transport from central Stockholm. Utö offers a lively version of island life. There are plenty of places to walk, bathe and enjoy nature as well as bars and restaurants. However, the best way to start your day is with a trip to the bakery, where you'll have trouble deciding what to have for breakfast, before determining that you'll come back again later for fika.

If you want a more serene environment with fewer visitors, Svartsö is a good alternative and takes around two and a half hours to reach by boat from central Stockholm. Lying in the central area of the archipelago, the island is covered with trees and has several lakes. The best way to get around the island is by bicycle, which can be rented. Aside from the stunning nature, Svartsö has its own local shop and a well-regarded restaurant, Svartsö Krog, where the emphasis is on simple, good food.

If you don't have your own luxury yacht or a summer house, one easy way to find affordable accommodation in the archipelago is through STF (Svenska Turistföreningen) who are responsible for hostels throughout Sweden. There are a range of different types of accommodation, from private rooms with their own bathrooms through to shared rooms and you can usually rent bedding if you don't want to bring your own. The hostels are typically clean and well kept, but alternatively you can just bring your tent and camp wherever the mood takes you. Some islands are only accessible in the summer, so it pays to check before you set sail!

42. Take A Boat Trip To Fjäderholmarna

"Ska vi ta en snabbtur I skärgården?"
Should we take a quick trip to the archipelago?

If you don't have time to spend a few days on a trip out to the archipelago, then Fjäderholmarna is an absolute must (depending on the time of year). It takes less than half an hour by boat to reach Fjäderholmarna from central Stockholm, yet it is an opportunity to

>TOURIST

experience a real taste of life in the archipelago, which Stockholmers love so much for good reason.

The island is relatively small and is fun to walk around as you come across various bars, cafes, little shops and great view points as you go round. Some parts of the islands are more lively, but equally it's usually possible to find a quieter place to have a picnic and a swim.

If you are in the mood for something more upmarket, Fjaderholmarnas Krog offers luxury dining in a luxury environment. Regardless of the weather you are guaranteed an excellent view out to sea while you enjoy fine cuisine. It also has a fireplace and armchairs inside for those chillier days.

Boats run regularly from several places in Stockholm, and run quite late into the evening, meaning there is no need to rush back to the city.

43. See The Fortress At Vaxholm

"Se upp för kanonkulorna"
Watch out for the cannon balls

Vaxholm is a city (in name, not size) located in Stockholm's archipelago. It is accessible all year round by road as well as boat, but it's more fun to go by boat and takes about an hour from central Stockholm.

Laura Andrews

Vaxholm is a beautiful city to walk around and enjoy, with cobbled streets and colourfully painted, old wooden houses, it feels quite different to walking around Stockholm city centre. Vaxholm is also known for its interesting shops and has a number of great restaurants and cafes.

The most famous sight is Vaxholm fortress, originally constructed to defend Stockholm from attacks by sea and having successfully fought off attacks from the Danish and the Russians hundreds of years ago, it is now an informative museum. It stands on its own island and is good for a little visit if you're interested in history.

44. Fika With A History At Vete-Katten And Gunnarsons

"Ska vi ha bullar eller praliner, eller varför inte båda?"
Should we have buns or pralines, or why not both?

Why not enjoy some history as well as the fika at two of the oldest cafes in Stockholm. Here you will always find tourists and locals alike.

Vete-Katten, located on Kungsgatan 55 in Norrmalm, was founded in 1928 by Ester Nordhammar and employed only young women until 1961. Vete-Katten serves breakfast, lunch and, on Tuesdays, afternoon tea, but it's the sweet treats that are the star attraction. If you're tired of

>TOURIST

eating cinnamon buns (as if that could ever happen) then you can opt for Vete-Katten's prestigious pralines. These are hand made by the owner himself, Johan Sandelin, confectioner and award winning pastry chef. Vete-Katten is always busy, but is surprisingly large and it's usually possible to find somewhere to sit.

Gunnarsons is on Götgatan 22 in Södermalm, it was founded in 1946 and is still family run. You will not be disappointed by the range of bread, cakes and buns. Gunnarsons also has its own range of pralines, each painstakingly made by hand by their team of confectioners. In the summer you can get home-made ice cream, including their special saffron ice cream. Like Vete-Katten, Gunnarsons has a large interior, so even on the busy days, it's usually possible to find a place.

45. Spice Things Up With Two Thai Restaurants

"Jag vill ha extra chilli"
I would like extra chilli

Once you've eaten all the Swedish food you can manage, you're craving something with a bit of spice, that hasn't been pickled, and you're tired of stylish and minimalist restaurant designs, there are a number of good Thai restaurants in Stockholm that are brimming with a decidedly un-Swedish atmosphere.

Laura Andrews

Moored in the water to the south of Södermalm at Kajplats 301, Norra Hammarbyhamnen, you will find Thai Boat, which is exactly as it sounds. A Thai restaurant, on a boat. In the summer this is a fun, lively place to enjoy the sun, while in the winter they have a wood burning stove, surrounded by sofas and armchairs covered with furs, creating the perfect cosy winter ambiance.

If you're looking to escape Sweden even more, you can try Koh Phangan. There's two locations, one in Östermalm (Nybrogatan 8) and one in Södermalm (Skånegatan 57). As you step inside you will be immediately transported to the Thai rainforest, thunderstorms included, with fairy lights and lanterns galore. Watch out for the fish swimming through the streams between tables as you make your way over bridges and around trees to your seat.

As a word of warning, if you've been asking for extra chilli everywhere you go, you'll have noticed that Swedish food, even the stuff labelled as being hot, isn't very hot. However, when you ask for extra chilli at a Thai restaurant, with Thai chefs, you'll get Thai style extra chilli, and it will be hot!

>TOURIST

46. Do Saturday Night Like A Swede

"Skål!"
Cheers!

Going out to bars and clubs in Northern Europe can be a very different experience to some of its more southerly counterparts, Sweden perhaps even more so. Alcohol in Sweden is heavily regulated and outside of bars and restaurants, the only place you can buy alcohol is in the state owned shop, Systembolaget. The concept behind Systembolaget is that it helps reduce problems caused by alcohol for both individuals and society, as alcohol is sold responsibly rather than as a means to make a profit.

You need to be 18 to be served alcohol in a bar in Sweden, but you must be at least 20 to buy alcohol from Systembolaget. If you plan on browsing the shelves, be aware of the opening hours, with most Systembolaget stores closing at around 6 or 7pm, with shorter opening hours on Saturdays. It is not open at all on Sundays and there are restricted opening hours around many public holidays.

Drinking alcohol is expensive in Stockholm and, as a result, many people choose to gather at friends' houses to have a few drinks before hitting the clubs. This means that it can be pretty quiet out until much later on in the evening, also meaning that going out earlier is an ideal way to avoid queues and entrance fees to clubs.

Laura Andrews

47. Buy Souvenirs

"Jag vill köpa en souvenir"
I want to buy a souvenir

The main shopping street in Stockholm is Drottninggatan (Queen's Street), located in Norrmalm. Here you will find everything from typical high-street stores to souvenir shops and many, many H&M stores. It is also usually incredibly crowded and normally avoided at all costs by Stockholm's residents, but an easy place to buy some souvenirs.

If you're looking to do some serious shopping, but don't want the hassle of fighting your way through the crowds in Drottninggatan, you can head north to The Mall of Scandinavia, located in Solna. It is the second largest mall of all the Nordic countries as well as home to Sweden's first IMAX cinema. They quite often also have pop-up shops and other seasonal events.

For a taste of the luxury, designer shops can be found in the Stureplan area, while Stockholm's answer to Harrod's, department store NK, which was founded in 1902, is situated at nearby Kungsträdgården.

For an extensive range of souvenirs, from Viking hats to moose-shaped cheese slicers, be sure to hit the souvenir shops in Gamla Stan. These are particularly good at Christmas when you can buy all manner of decorative tomte and light-up Christmas stars.

>TOURIST

If you are not really into shopping but want something identifiably Swedish to have in your home, stop by the shop Design Torget, which can be found in several places, including Arlanda airport. Sweden is known for its design and Design Torget selects products from both known and unknown Swedish designers, giving you the opportunity to bring a bit of scandi minimalist cool to your own home at an affordable price. You won't find one Stockholmer who doesn't own something from Design Torget.

48. Learn Something For Free At One Of Many Museums

"Tiden räcker inte för att se alla museum!"
There isn't time to visit all these museums!

Many state-owned museums in Sweden are currently free to visit so forget the usual admission-charging tourist favourites such as the Vasa museum and the ABBA museum (well, maybe don't forget them, but just put them to the back of your mind for a bit) and head to one of the many free museums in Stockholm.

These include, to name but a few, the modern museum (modern and contemporary art), army museum (the history of war from the perspective of a country that hasn't been at war for over 200 years),

Laura Andrews

Swedish history museum (Vikings), Skokloster Castle (Baroque castle outside Stockholm), the medieval museum (medieval history of Stockholm including an underground exhibition of the original 16th century town wall), the Hallwyl museum (luxury, palatial-style home built at the end of the 1800s), the royal armoury (the history of Sweden's monarchs through their clothing), the Swedish museum of natural history (including a Swedish nature exhibition), the national maritime museum (Swedish ships), ArkDes (architecture and design) and the national sports museum of Sweden (history of sports in Sweden and, yes, they apparently do play sports other than hockey).

49. Embrace Your Inner Tourist

"Ta med kartan och kameran"
Get the map and the camera ready

If you do want to have some typical Stockholm tourist boxes checked off your list, here are some key, but also good, tourist activities:

Even locals will tell you they've visited the Vasa museum, they'll also recommend it to you the second you step foot in town. Here you will find the Vasa warship, almost in its entirety. The ship sunk on its maiden voyage in 1628 and was found again in the 1950s having been preserved by the cold, brackish water.

>TOURIST

The Nordic Museum is Sweden's largest museum of cultural history and has a range of different types of exhibition encompassing all areas of Swedish life and history.

The royal palace is one of the largest in Europe and is the official residence of the King of Sweden. If you like royal palaces, this one doesn't disappoint.

Skyview takes you up to the top of the Ericsson Globe, the world's largest spherical building, offering fantastic views of the city. The trip takes about half an hour.

Laura Andrews

50. Learn Swedish

"Pratar du svenska? - Ja, lite"
Do you speak swedish? - Yes, a little

As most Swedes speak perfect English, there's no need to use your language-learning energy on the usual tourist stuff, so why not impress with these opportunistic phrases and classic Swedish sayings?

Swedish	Pronunciation Help	English
Lycka till!	Look-a till!	Good luck!
Varken för mycket eller för litet, bara lagom	Var-ken fur mi-cket eller fur lee-tet, bara largom	Neither too much nor too little, just right
Ska vi fika?	Scar vee fee-kah?	Should we have coffee and cake?
Jag drar på semester nu, vi ses om en månad	Yarg drar pour semester noo, vee sez om en monad	I'm going on holiday now, see you in a month
Det finns inget dåligt väder, bara dåliga kläder	Det finns inget door-ligt vedder, bar-a door-ligt kledder	There's no such thing as bad weather, only the wrong clothes
Jag bor på Grand Hotel	Yarg bore pour Grand Hotel	I am staying at the Grand Hotel
Var ligger Arlanda-Expressen?	Var ligger Arlanda-Expressen?	Which way is the Arlanda Express?
Jag vill köpa en sjudagarsbiljett, tack	Yarg vill shurp-ah en shoodargs-billy-ett, tack	I would like to buy a seven-day ticket please
Jag skulle vilja hyra ett par skridskor	Yarg skool-uh vil-ya he-yrah ett par skreed-skor	I would like to hire a pair of ice skates

>TOURIST

Tiden räcker inte för att se alla museum!	Tee-den recker inter fur at ser al-ah museum!	There isn't time to visit all these museums!
Äter bör man, annars dör man	Eh-ter bur man, annars dur man	One should eat, otherwise one will die
Kan du rekommenderar en god cocktail?	Can doo recomend-air-rah en gooed cocktail?	Can you recommend a good cocktail?
Låt oss softa med en kopp kaffe	Lort oss soft-ah med en cop caf-feh	Let's chill with a cup of coffee
Oj! Jag tror att jag såg ett spöke!	Oi! Yarg traw at yarg sawg ett spurk-uh	Oh! I think I saw a ghost!
Jag vill ha toast skagen och köttbullar, tack	Yarg vil har toast skargen ock shirt-bull-ar, tack	I will have prawns on toast and meatballs please
Så många kyrkor och hipsters har jag aldrig sett	So mong-ah shirk-or ock hipster har yarg al-drig set	I have never seen so many churches and hipsters
Titta! En häst gömmer sig där!	Titt-ah! En hest yurm-uh say dair!	Look! There's a horse hiding there!
Lite frisk luft har ingen dött av	Leet-ah frisk lurft har ingen durt ahv	A bit of fresh air never killed anyone
Vilken film vill du se?	Vee-ken film vil doo sair?	What film do you want to see?
Vilken härlig frunch buffé!	Vee-ken hair-lig fr-uh-nch buffet!	What a lovely brunch buffet!
Vilken vacker utställning!	Vee-ken vack-uh oot-stellning	What a beautiful exhibition!
Jag aldrig ätit så här god vegetarisk mat	Yarg al-drig et-it so hair gooed vegg-eh-tar-isk mart	I never thought vegetarian food could be so good
Det är som att resa	Det air some at ray-sa	It's like going back

Laura Andrews

tillbaka i tiden	till-bark-ah i teeden	in time
Oj, vilken fin utsikt!	Oi, vee-ken feen oot-sickt	Wow, what a great view!
Smaklig måltid	Smark-leeg maul-teed	Enjoy your meal
Det är skönt att vi bara besöka fängelset!	Det air shernt at vee bara buh-serka feng-el-set	It's nice that we're only visiting the prison!
Behöver jag klättringutrustning? - Nej, bara fika	Buh-hurver yarg klettring oot-truhst-ning? - Nay, bara fee-kah	Do I need climbing equipment? - No, just fika
Vänta! Jag måste ta en bild	Vent-ah! Yarg mosst-eh tar en bild	Wait! I must take a picture
Är det Benny som äger det här hotellet?	Air det Benny som air-ger det hair hotellet?	Is it Benny who owns this hotel?
Morgonstund har guld i mun	Morgon-stund har goold i mun	The early bird catches the worm
Tio spänn på att jag kommer vinna	Tee-oh spenn pour at yarg commer vinn-ah	I bet ten bucks that I will win
Oj, vad många trappor!	Oi, vard monga trap-or	Oh, what a lot of stairs!
Detta är nog min favoritplats	Dett-ah air norg min far-vor-it-platts	This might be one of my favourite places
Ska vi ta en strand promenad?	Scar vee tar en strand promenard?	Shall we take a walk by the water?
Här skiner alltid solen	Hair sheener al-teed soul-en	Here the sun is always shining
Vilken typ av blommar är detta?	Vee-ken teep arv bloomar air dett-ah?	Which type of flowers are these?
Titta på björnen!	Titt-ah pour byurn-en!	Look at the bear!
Det här är mitt	Det hair air mitt far-	They are my

>TOURIST

favoritband!	vor-it-band!	favourite band!
Vill du dela?	Vill doo dair-lah	Do you want to share?
Ska vi mingla i baren?	Scar vee mingl-ah ee bar-en?	Should we go and mingle in the bar?
I Stockholm finns naturen alltid nära	I Stockholm finns natt-ooren al-teed nair-ah	In Stockholm, the nature is always nearby
Har du packat smörgåsar och fika?	Har doo pack-at smurg-oss-ar ock fee-kah?	Have you packed the sandwiches and fika?
Med solkräm och badkläder är vi redo	Med sol-creme ock bard-klairder air vee rairdo	We've got sun cream and swimwear, now we're ready
Ska vi ta en snabbtur i skärgården?	Scar vee tar en snabb-tur i shair-gorden?	Should we take a short trip to the archipelago?
Se upp för kanonkulorna!	Sair uhp fur canoon-cool-ornah!	Watch out for the cannon balls!
Ska vi ha bullar eller praliner, eller varför inte båda?	Scar vee har bull-ar eller prar-leener, eller var-fur inter bourd-ah	Shall we have buns or pralines, or why not both?
Jag vill ha extra chilli	Yarg vill har extra shilli	I would like extra chilli
Skål!	Skawl	Cheers!
Jag vill köpa en souvenir	Yarg vill shurp-ah en souvenir	I want to buy a souvenir
Ta med kartan och kameran	Tar med car-tan ock car-meran	Get the map and the camera ready
Pratar du svenska? – Ja, lite	Prart-ar doo svenska? - yar, leet-eh	Do you speak Swedish? - Yes, a little

75

Laura Andrews

>TOURIST

TOP REASONS TO BOOK THIS TRIP

Variety: culture, history, food and nature, there's something for everyone

Views: wherever you go you stumble across another stunning view

Fika: the excuse to eat cake wherever you go as it's part of the culture

Water: boats, bathing and blue everywhere; the water defines the city

Nature: you're never far away from a green or blue space

Time: the sooner you visit, the sooner you can make your permanent move

Laura Andrews

> TOURIST
GREATER THAN A TOURIST

Visit GreaterThanATourist.com:
http://GreaterThanATourist.com

Sign up for the Greater Than a Tourist Newsletter:
http://eepurl.com/cxspyf

Follow us on Facebook:
https://www.facebook.com/GreaterThanATourist

Follow us on Pinterest:
http://pinterest.com/GreaterThanATourist

Follow us on Instagram:
http://Instagram.com/GreaterThanATourist

Laura Andrews

> TOURIST
GREATER THAN A TOURIST

Please leave your honest review of this book on Amazon and Goodreads. Thank you. We appreciate your positive and constructive feedback. Thank you.

Laura Andrews

NOTES